Mr.
Tries Again

Written by Sarah Prince
Illustrated by Peter Paul Bajer

® sundance™
A Haights Cross Communications ™ Company

I am the big, bad wolf.

The very big, very bad wolf.

I have a new plan.

I am going to catch
the three little pigs.

"Little pigs, little pigs,
let me come in!"

"Not by the hair
on our chinny chin chins,"
said the three little pigs.

"Little pigs, little pigs,
let me come in!
Or I'll bash, and I'll crash,
and I'll smash your house in."

RW 68

4

5

So, I bashed, and I crashed,

but I could not smash the house in.

RW87 7

"Little pigs, little pigs,
let me come in!"

"Not by the hair
on our chinny chin chins,"
said the three little pigs.

"Little pigs, little pigs,
let me come in!
Or I'll bash, and I'll crash,
and I'll smash your house in."

THUMP

9

So, I bashed, and I crashed,

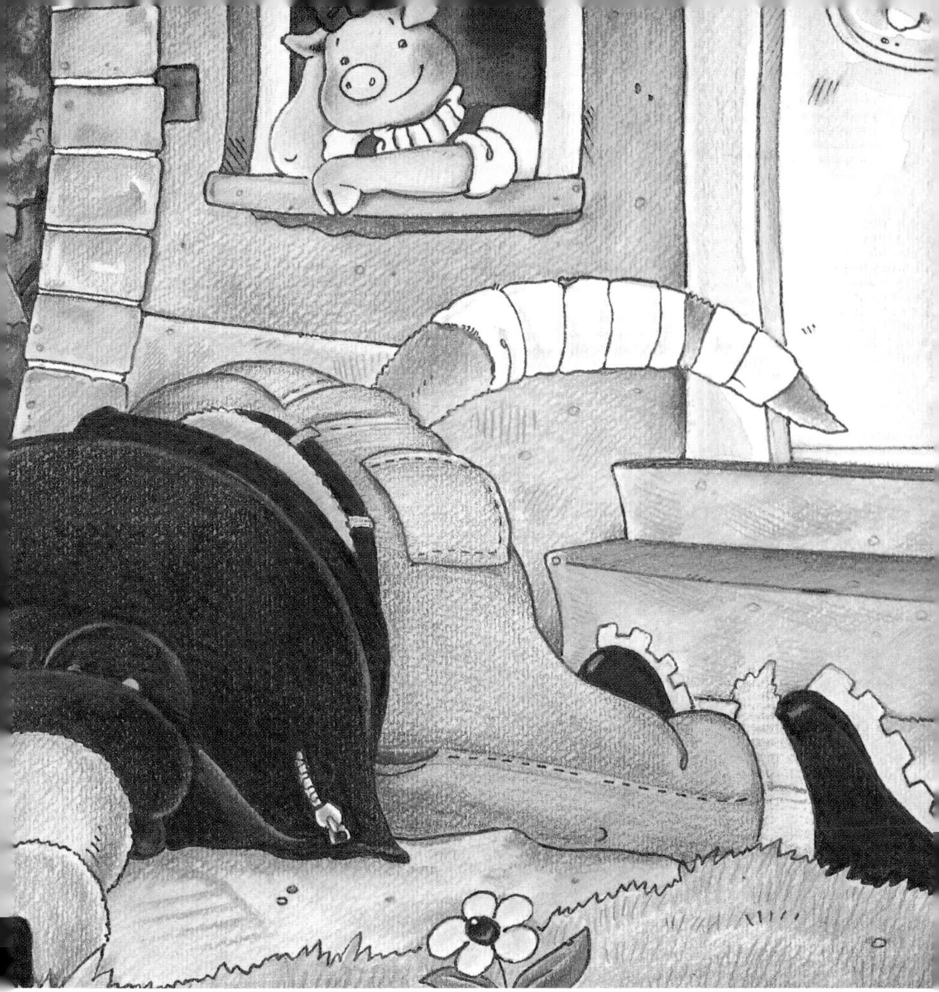

but I could not smash the house in.

"Little pigs, little pigs,
let me come in!"

"Not by the hair
on our chinny chin chins,"
said the three little pigs.

"Little pigs, little pigs,
let me come in!
Or I'll bash, and I'll crash,
and I'll smash your house in."

I ran up to the door.

I ran through the house.
I ran out the back door,
and I fell down the steps.

Bash!
Crash!
Smash!
Yeow!

15

"Ouch! My poor, poor head,"
I said.
"But I'll be back."